THE BEAUTIFUL EMPOWERED

PURPOSE DRIVEN

WOMAN

Fingerprints Of Beauty

Ollie M. & Freeman

© Copyright - Ollie M. & Freeman

Reprinted 2018, first printed in paperback 2010

ISBN: 10 - 0-971-5457-2-3

ISBN:13 - 978-0-9715457-2-4

Printed in the United States of America

All scriptures are taken from the King James Version of the
Holy Bible.

Edited by: Sheliawritesbooks

Cover Designed by MMADHOUSE Media

Manufactured in the United States of America

For information regarding discounts for bulk purchases, please
write to: P. O. Box 26223, St. Louis, MO 63136. You may also
email the author at: biblos2@ yahoo.com or call **314-741-9337**

Printed in United States of America

FREEMAN / NEW LIFE PRODUCTION
Florissant, Missouri 63033

CONTENTS

Dedication

This book is dedicated to all the women who have suffered and struggled to make this world a better place in which to live, and to the woman that is striving to be a pillar in her family, community, and nation.

Adorn me beautifully with the Jewels Of Life—
Hang an ornament of Love round my neck with
Beads of Care, Joy, Peace, and Gentleness.

Adorn me beautifully with the Jewels Of Life—
Crown my head with jewels, gems of
Humility,Equity, and Justice.

Adorn me beautifully with the Jewels Of Life—
Beautify me not with tangibles, but with the
Intangible precious stone of a life well lived;
Orchestrated from the heart, beautifully.

Ollie M. & Freeman

The Purpose Driven Woman

Beautiful, purpose driven, and empowered,
The lifeblood of feminity—
The power of motherhood—pillar of the family,
The icon of humankind.

The feminine flame of warmth and affection—
The embodiment of soul and spirit—
From birth to giving birth—
The grapevine of progeny,
The ripened, sweetened fruit of life,
From generation to generation.

The music enjoyed by men—
An orchestra of strings, finely tuned,
An instrument of beauty—
Purpose to perform, a masterpiece
Empowered by the breath of God—
Woman.

I was born with a purpose,
I live with a purpose,
I am purpose driven.
I am ready for the task of life.
I pursue my goals,
I am challenged, but not defeated,
I have a purpose, a dream, a conviction,
And the power to overcome.

[10]Who can find a virtuous woman? for her price is far above rubies.

[11]The heart of her husband doth safely trust in her, so that he shall have no need of spoil.

[12]She will do him good and not evil all the days of her life.

[13]She seeketh wool, and flax, and worketh willingly with her hands.

[14]She is like the merchants' ships; she bringeth her food from afar.

[15]She riseth also while it is yet night, and giveth meat to her household, and a portion to her maidens.

[16]She considereth a field, and buyeth it: with the fruit of her hands she planteth a vineyard.

[17]She girdeth her loins with strength, and strengtheneth her arms.

[18]She perceiveth that her merchandise is good: her candle goeth not out by night.

[19]She layeth her hands to the spindle, and her hands hold the distaff.

[20]She stretcheth out her hand to the poor; yea, she reacheth forth her hands to the needy.

[21]She is not afraid of the snow for her household: for all her household are clothed with scarlet.

[22]She maketh herself coverings of tapestry; her clothing is silk and purple.

²³Her husband is known in the gates, when he sitteth among the elders of the land.

²⁴She maketh fine linen, and selleth it; and delivereth girdles unto the merchant.

²⁵Strength and honour are her clothing; and she shall rejoice in time to come.

²⁶She openeth her mouth with wisdom; and in her tongue is the law of kindness.

²⁷She looketh well to the ways of her household, and eateth not the bread of idleness.

²⁸Her children arise up, and call her blessed; her husband also, and he praiseth her.

²⁹Many daughters have done virtuously, but thou excellest them all.

³⁰Favour is deceitful, and beauty is vain: but a woman that feareth the LORD, she shall be praised.

³¹Give her of the fruit of her hands; and let her own works praise her in the gates.

Proverbs 31:10-31King James Version (KJV)

THE EMPOWERED WOMAN

I am the empowered, purpose driven woman,
I am beautifully adorned with strength, tenacity,
And fortitude—I am a woman of character.

I am the President of my life,
Governor of my mind and heart,
Senator of my ways,
Mayor of my courage,
CEO of my actions,
Princess of good conduct,
Queen of my family.

I am the empowered, purpose driven woman,
I am rich in humility—beautiful in character,
I am an ambassador of dignity—
I am a conqueror of fear and doubt,
I am the Empowered, Purpose Driven Woman.

I AM WOMAN

I am woman—
Feminine pure—
Full of personality,
I am woman—
Complex and modest,
I am woman—
I am woman, I said!
I am woman—
Gracefully endowed by nature,
A sculpture of beauty,
A source of strength and love—I AM WOMAN.

INTRODUCTION

<u>THE BEAUTIFUL EMPOWERED PURPOSE DRIVEN WOM-AN</u> is a mild mannered tribute to the inward beauty of those women that possess the summum bonum of the terrestrial with flaming, vivid, radiant rays of empowerment of the celestial—earthly angels.

This book is my perspective of a powerful, purpose driven woman, and the intrinsic good that makes her beautiful. It is an eye-opener into the very characteristics that set her apart from other women that fall short of her blessed endowments.

In contemplating the inner and outer mechanics of a beautiful, powerful, and purpose driven specimen of God's creation, I had to rely heavily upon my culinary skills that took me to the kitchen of my reasoning to cook up a recipe fit for a queen; but yet acceptable by the masses of women and men who may read this book of the twenty-first century revealing the beauty of woman. Or, who may use this very book as a manual to unlock secret passages into the very realm of her beauty, in order to manipulate those beautiful innate characteristics, as well as acquired qualities.

The task of producing this book into print took me on a short adventure to the mountain of speculation. I had to focus my attention on the things that make a woman beautiful, powerful, and purpose driven, and how she plays her roles in the family, community, and the world.

I have not tried to unleash any hidden powers or formulate anything that would make her more than what she really is or by no means use my imagination to present a fictitious character that does not exist on (earth) terra firma.

This book is my personal perspective of who beautiful women are in the midst of women of diverse characteristics, social statuses, and personalities—considerations have been taken in a microscopic sense of looking at those intrinsic things so often overlooked, and not perceived by spectators.

In a glance, this book is an unfolding of truths that have shrouded the female through the birth pains of her entire being, from her primitive smothered slave type of existence, to her blazing as a radiant star in the firmament of human existence.

I was now in the "kitchen" of my mind, standing poised over my reasoning; I had to be a very skilled chef de cuisine; I mean a top of the line (topmost) cook, with a sense of what it takes to make this (book) stew just right. I had virtually to hone my skills. It was like weighing each grain of salt, counting each piece of ground pepper with a highly sensitive trained nose that could sense the slightest defect in each added ingredient. It is because I was aware that all women were not the same, and by no means was there any real life perfect comparison. I could have perused pages of history in search of the perfect woman, or just contemplated the women of my own roots that led to my meager existence. But, since I am a product of both male and female, it would have been unfair to leave out the contributions of the good qualities of nurture and nature from both parents.

While contemplating the very essence of the empowered, purpose driven woman's beauty, I had to search deeply within myself. Like Sherlock Holmes, I couldn't let a single clue escape my probing. There had to be evidence—there had to be *fingerprints of beauty*. While I did frequent inward searches, like the paparazzi, I was ready at all times to take notes from the multitude of women that made their performance of life noticeable on the stage of human existence.

I knew for a start, that some women possess that thing I coined, "Fingerprints of Beauty." Others were likely not to have any underlying well-defined qualities: for I knew women could be your worst nightmare. On the other hand, you might find them soothing like the "Balm in Gilead" that makes the wounded glad.

I welcome you to my table. Each plate is filled with delicacy. A fork is to the left and a dessert spoon is to the right. A napkin is neatly folded, and I am your connoisseur and chef. Behold the *Beautiful, Empowered, Purpose Driven Woman*.

A SPECIAL TRIBUTE TO MY LIFE

I was attuned to the dynamics of my own pilgrimage of life. I wanted my life to serve as a paradigm of success and beauty, overlaid with pure virtues. While on the other hand, I was striving to be a paragon of righteous living, attuned spiritually to the higher power of God, inseparable from His overshadowing beauty, grandeur, and majesty.

I had longed to be a wise pedagogue with a keen sense of the aesthetics of life. . . I stood poised on the mountain of speculation. From my plateau, I sorted the beatitudes as they danced graciously in the valley below. Blessed are the "Pure In Heart" made her advance first. She tugged at my inner self and pierced my heart with purity. She led the way for the next of her kin: Blessed are the "Poor In Spirit." She was a glorious example of humility that persuaded me to take a good look at arrogance, opulence of spirit, and what measures they would deal to me. From where I stood, I noticed the other beatitudes—they gloriously blessed my heart and mind.

⁴Blessed are those who mourn, for they will be comforted. ⁵ Blessed are the meek, for they will inherit the earth. ⁶ Blessed are those who hunger and thirst for righteousness, for they will be filled. ⁷ Blessed are the merciful, for they will be shown mercy. ⁸ Blessed are the pure in heart, for they will see God. ⁹ Blessed are the peacemakers, for they will be called children of God. (St. Matthew 5:4-8)

The perimeter of my life was now set by my spirit, leaving me no room to venture beyond decency. My soul was permeated with an exploding sense of a higher inner self, a spiritual connection, and a super awareness that supplied the frailness of my being with the needed strength for my plight of life.

Life is complex, and I needed a good portion of perspicacity all stirred in a mixture of sagacity.

I made my heart beautiful with philanthropy and I strengthened my arms by flexing the muscles of sharing and caring. . . .

I wanted that perfect photo that would make my life a picturesque panorama of beauty, a spectacle for all the good people that had to travel the road of life with me. While ruminating over my path of life, I said others must be able to take notice of my life, not because of my words alone, but by observing the painting on the wall; that is, not for its beauty, but for its truth portrayed by the life I had lived.

Piety was my pipe and I had to smoke it each day. Rising early for that morning smoke and going to bed with it snugly tucked away in my mind.

I closed my eyes with a sincere prayer and rehearsed my favorite numbers of Psalms. Then, while my head rested on my pillow, I would dream of a new day when I could arise and carry on my rituals of beauty, habits from the soul.

My stand in life would be didactic, purpose to the establishment of womanhood—fiery trails would present themselves like ravenous wolves, but I had to persevere and I remained sanguine with hopes of someday receiving glorious accolades.

I had arrived at the peak of my endeavors. My superlative skills as a woman of dignity, depths, heights, width, warmth, wisdom, and knowledge was only a mere drop in the bucket; there were still more knowledge, wisdom, understanding, and virtue in the *fountain of life* for me to draw out and imbibe.

A Special Song

Ollie M. & Freeman
His Eye Is On the Sparrow

My Favorite Psalms

¹The Lord is my shepherd; I shall not want. ²He maketh me to lie down in green pastures: he leadeth me beside the still waters. ³He restoreth my soul: he leadeth me in the paths of righteousness for his name's sake. ⁴Yea, though I walk through the valley of the shadow of death, I will fear no evil: for thou art with me; thy rod and thy staff they comfort me. ⁵Thou preparest a table before me in the presence of mine enemies: thou anointest my head with oil; my cup runneth over. ⁶Surely goodness and mercy shall follow me all the days of my life: and I will dwell in the house of the Lord forever. (23ʳᵈ Psalm)

My Favorite Scripture

For verily I say unto you, That whosoever shall say unto this mountain, Be thou removed, and be thou cast into the sea; and shall not doubt in his heart, but shall believe that those things which he saith shall come to pass; he shall have whatsoever he saith (St. Mark 11:23).

The Beautiful Empowered Purpose Driven Woman

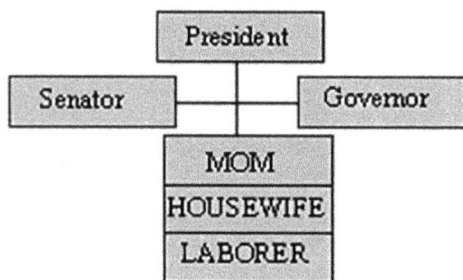

Focused

In Control

Purpose Driven

Beautiful

Powerful
Ready for the Task
Willing To Endure

Steadfast and Determined

Enthusiastic

	President	
Senator		Governor
	MOM	
	HOUSEWIFE	
	LABORER	

Say unto wisdom, Thou art my sister; and call
Understanding thy kinswoman. Proverbs

12

CLUE I

BEAUTY / AESTHETICS
Unveil the sacred shroud of femininity, reveal to me the secrets of the beautiful woman—make me aware of aesthetics—let me see with my eyes, beauty—let me touch, beauty.

I had done my homework. The handwriting was on the wall, that which would be weighed in the balance would either tip the scales in favor of the beauty of some women; and at the same time the balance would, for others, beckon for radical changes. These radical changes would raise their consciousness to new levels and totally renew their perspective of themselves and their purpose of life.

THE SEARCHING MODE — NATURE
All around me were beautiful things to observe. The moment was right, the dawning of a beautiful, serene, and cool June day made its arrival with all the makings of a masterpiece. Like skilled brush strokes of Leonardo da Vinci's masterpiece, the Mona Lisa, had once more appeared, engraving an image of beauty on the canvas of my mind. A masterpiece of nature's beauty had summoned me to speculate on a panorama display that flooded my already captivated, probing mind with inspiration in the purest sense of poetry. A rosebush presented itself as a bouquet with colorful new blossoms. Tulips stood like sentinels over a field of zoysia grass that made obeisance, bowing down by the gentle touch of a southern breeze. I saw a honeysuckle lend the grace of its stems to resting butterflies—it was all so beautiful. Just in the reach of my hands, honeybees nourished themselves on the nectar of inviting flowers; a hummingbird in midair, fanning its wings over three thousand times per minute, hovering between the terra firma, and blossoms of elegantly colored flowers, rich with an inviting sweet nectar. It was the essence of nature, engraving on my mind an awareness (insight)

of what was undefiled and beautiful.

The search was on. I was a spectator, a beholder, and I knew that there were many beautiful things to catch my eyes. But in the hustle and bustle of a busy, almost never ending demanding day, I had to apply what I coined as "life's brakes," stopping to take a few quiet moments for myself. These quiet moments would give me the needed time for introspection, speculation, meditation, and above all, time to launch an intense search for what makes woman the queen of the species. I was determined to find the time, the place, and the inner consciousness to inhale breaths of inspirations, capturing the subtle, unfounded beauty of each progressing moment.

I wanted to know the real meaning and purpose of my life and what it had to offer me, as well as what I had to offer others from what I supposed, humble beginnings. My garden of (Eden) life with all its grandeur, complexity, and simplicity provided me space and time to unveil its secrets of beauty, success, and power. But life (Eden) is not without its uninvited and unwelcome ugly social scars, culprits of a sick society. In my (life) Eden, I am a significant little stitch in the tapestry of life; a tiny, but significant, flower in the midst of myriads.

I am a flower
In the garden of creation,
I blossom with womanhood,
I am a rose, a bouquet of femininity—
I am a flower, one in many,
Gracefully endowed—
I am a flower,
My fragrances I spread,
My nectar is sweet,
I am a FLOWER.

A SENSE OF BEING

In the midst of a chaotic world, I had to find the very things that make me who I am, and bestow upon me qualities that make me a beautiful, firmly established female creature. I am, I am, I said! I am unique. I'm here, and I am a woman. However, I wanted to define woman in a real life sense of knowing what she is, by who I am. I wanted to paint a portrait of my inner self.

I AM SO I AM

I am here, I exist in body,
Mind, and soul—
I am so I am,
A woman indeed, an entity
Of power, structured to reproduce
Offspring—humankind—
I am here, graciously,
I am so I am, feminine—woman.

***Profiling*—** I had to put together in my mind an image that best describes woman, a 360° perfect profile of the mass, labeled woman. I wanted to find out what's it like to be a beautiful, well-cultured woman or even one that has been neglected or abused. Profound rhetorical questions swept through my mind like a tornado, rooting up already preconceived ideas about the female gender, and my mind was flooded with concerns about the losses—the kind of losses some women suffer through neglect, abuse, and perhaps a bad relationship. I wanted to pinpoint her strengths and weaknesses, as well as define what is exclusively female by nature.

INTROSPECTION — SEARCHING FOR THE JEWELS

Discovering — I was now on the move, searching for the precious *"Jewels of Life."* The inward jewels that make a beautiful woman a creature to be greatly admired and appreciated in the sphere of fleshly beings.

THE SHIP OF REASONING

The ship of my mind had now left the dock of *inquiry*, launching me on a voyage of reasoning and discovery. I was the inquiring explorer sailing the seven seas of my mind. No hideous monster of doubt or the threats of hurricane proportioned winds of mental obstacles could stop me now. It was like saying, "All Aboard, Full Speed Ahead!"

The treasure chest containing life's beautiful jewels had to be found and opened. In it would be all the jewels that make beautiful women sparkle like diamonds of the highest quality, set in the finest gold, and engraved with the logo, "Purity." I would be rich with the kind of wealth that would cause both men and women to stop in awe, as they try to decipher my secrets of beauty and empowerment.

I was on an eye-opening adventure sailing toward the dawning of self-discovery, looking inwardly, discovering what was to be the prize keystone that held each stone of self-worth in place. First, I knew that the outward appearance wasn't a true reflection of the inner entity that lives inside this earthly house of flesh and bones.

The adorning of my physical body (earthly house) enhances my appearance to others but, by all means, it is not the outward adorning, the wearing of earrings, bracelets, beads, and other jewels that makes me who I am. Perhaps, the old adage is true, "Beauty is in the eye of the beholder." Yet, there is another wise saying, "Beauty is only skin deep." Both of these adages hold a pinch of truth; but I am more concerned about the inner (beauties) mechanisms that would transform my outward appearance into a beautiful portrait without any outward adorning.

SEARCH FOR INWARD TREASURES

From The Inside Out — Beauty from within, the imponderable bouquet of a pure spirit, a stable mind, and a good heart, had to be a win-win combination that would land me on the island of self-discovery and quench that burning insatiable desire for: awareness, knowledge, wisdom, and understanding—my ship of reasoning had now docked at the port of enlightenment.

Drawing Up A Parallelism — Opening the Treasure Chest of Life would bring me a little closer to a real sense of beauty. Each piece of jewelry would be precious—I wanted a keen sense of what each piece meant to me—the light broke forth—there it was, at my disposal: the "Treasure Chest of Life;" the only thing I had to do was lift the lid and place my hands on those things that summoned my attention. I went for the gold. "The Gold Rush Was On."

The Treasure Chest of Life's beauty was now mine for the taking, but before I could open the lid, I summoned my sister, Wisdom, and my kinswoman, Understanding—I went for the gold.

THE GOLD RUSH — The Gold Ring

The glimmer of a gold ring on my finger gave me a sense of owning something that was real and valuable, versus the unreal; but I needed the beauty of gold within me.

A golden ring within my soul was a must; the circle would represent a never-ending cycle of being true to myself. It also represented to me the kind of faith and fortitude that would be least tarnished by unpleasant life events. Yet, I understood that even gold had a smelting point, but to be like it meant holding a kind of luster in my heart that would give me an edge in times of difficulties.

GOLD (chemical symbol Au, atomic number 79), a dense, lustrous, yellow, malleable metal that is least tarnished by wear and tear—virtually indestructible (Encyclopedia Britannica).

GOLD A POWERFUL FAITH

That the trial of your faith, being much more precious than of gold that perisheth, though it be tried with fire, might be found unto praise and honour and glory at the appearing of Jesus Christ (I Peter 1:7).

THE GOLD DIFFERENCE — Gold would make the difference, and I would continue to be radiantly beautiful even after being tried by fire. But in a larger sense, I had to reassure myself of the pure quality of gold that made me who I am. I also had to know when I was presenting to myself truths that would make me complete. I could be strong, empowered, and beautiful today; but perhaps tomorrow's tests and trials would leave me shipwrecked, busted, and disgusted with myself and others.

GOLD OF SELF-WORTH — SELF-ESTEEM

I had to value those inward gold nuggets for without real value within, my perspective of self-worth would leave me with a warp sided opinion of who I really was—gold was a must! But the Treasure Chest of Life had more than gold to offer.

MY EYES ARE ON THE DIAMONDS

I had to see beyond the gold of self-worth, and delightfully place my hands on the diamonds. Diamonds are precious stones, and I had to have them sparkling from within my very being, making my inward character sparkle like diamonds of the finest quality. These inner gemstones of life's beauty are a must. I could not afford not to have them set graciously in my heart, and mind, making up the kind of "diamond" personality that sparkles even in the midst of adversity, distress, or even neglect.

BE A DIAMOND AMONG WOMEN

DIAMONDS ARE A GIRL'S BEST FRIEND

What woman would not appreciate a cluster of high graded diamonds? Diamonds are minerals composed of pure carbon, the hardest natural substance known and are valuable gemstones. They are minerals with refractive power, varying from colorless to black. (*Encyclopedia Britannica*).

DIAMOND

*O beautiful diamond of intrinsic
Beauty, fill my heart and mind.*

*O beautiful diamond of humility,
Sparkle from within my soul,
Make expressions of Meekness,
Gentleness and Kindness.*

*O beautiful diamond, a matchless
Gemstone of inner grace,
Endow me with splendor,
Make me a beautiful woman
Sparkling from within—
Diamond*

THE INNER BROOCH

The Inner Brooch—a beautiful pin created from gold and diamonds, a reflection of inner beauty, was now created forming the finest jewelry of my very being. The brooch of life consisted of the gold of faith and fortitude, inlaid with the precious gemstones of integrity, chastity, innocence, and humility. The Inner Brooch with its precious stones added to me virtues that made me more beautiful.

What more could a girl (lady) want? Yet, after plundering the Treasure Chest of Life for the gold and diamonds, my wandering eyes caught sight of the silver. The Treasure Chest of Life was apparently inexhaustible; and wisdom, the guardian of my common senses, would lead me to take as much as I pleased. It was my (life) time, my space, and my treasure. My adventurous voyage was paying off in great inward riches and, of course, I wanted enough inward wealth to share with other women who had not been as successful on their voyage of life; or had perhaps experienced a lot of misfortune, because they had failed to navigate the waves on life's tempestuous driven sea. Yes, I had a little gold and some diamonds that demanded a spectator's attention; but there was the Silver — Silver and Gold.

SILVER AND GOLD

"Silver and Gold," erupted from within my soul. I could hear an old church mother singing, "I'd rather have Jesus than silver and gold." But the very sense of what had made me a beautiful woman kept pressing the accelerator of my mind—just go for the silver.

SILVER — The luster of silver caught me in a web of speculation, it was not gold, but it was beautiful. It was not diamonds, but it sparkled, nonetheless. I held it close to my heart and searched for its meaning for inner beauty.

Silver: a metallic chemical element, one of the transition elements,
Chemical symbol Ag atomic number 47
It is a white, lustrous, precious metal, valued for its beauty.
It is also valued for its electrical conductivity, which is the
Highest of any metal (Encyclopedia Britannica)

Adding the Silver to the Gold and the Diamonds would by all

means make me richer and more beautiful than ever before, so I took the silver plunge and brought up the silver crown of *decency* and *self-respect*, and allowed it to become the conductor of the electricity of *innocence*, *piety*, and *chastity*.

Silver Tarnishes — Silver, although sparkling with luster, could easily tarnish, so I had to accept the facts of life, meaning that I could be up and beautiful today, but down, stained, and tarnished at the crowing of the cock. But to avoid tarnished silver; I had to be constant, alert, and keep the silver of life polished, that is, with the polish of a sound mind, while at the same time, I had to keep my feet firmly placed on a sure foundation. My pastor used to hammer out words of firm conviction, "On Christ the Solid Rock I Stand." Then he would put his finger behind his right ear and yell, "All other grounds are sinking sand." I would get chill bumps all over me knowing that somehow or someway, there was a sure foundation—I am empowered with a sure foundation.

ON LIFE'S RESTLESS SEA

On life's restless sea—though the sea billows, I dare not stop to succumb to its motions—I am a sailor, sailing. I have the power! I have the determination, and I have the faith—I will sail on. *"O restless sea of life, be calm today, for a sailor's delight; peace be upon the waters—peace be still, you raging waves of despair, for your churning billows will not deter my quest."*

ONBOARD THE SHIP OF LIFE

Onboard the Ship of Life I sail,
sailing with the anchors of faith, hope,
and charity, always keeping a watchful eye
for those whose vessels are battered by stormy
weather—to throw out the lifeline and
welcome them aboard.

Onboard the Ship of Life, sailing
toward the setting of the sun, until I reach
that beautiful shore where I shall feast
on eternal bliss, and live in peace
and harmony forevermore.

THERE—IN THE TREASURE CHEST OF LIFE---

RUBIES

Rubies! Rubies! I love rubies' transparent red corundum. Some rubies vary in color from deep to pale red, and some of them have a tinge of purple. I really love purple; it is the color of royalty—a queen you are, and a queen I am. After contemplating their worth, I saw a ruby that was pigeon-blood red; it was the most valuable. The red reminded me of the Savior's blood that covers my life—"I've been washed in the blood of the Lamb; and I am covered by the blood—all my sins are washed away."

Rubies are now part of what makes me beautiful. They are for the poor, the wretched, the outcast, the downtrodden, and yes, the rich who need beauty and empowerment.

Now that I had the Gold, Silver, Diamonds, and Rubies of a beautiful empowered life; I had become an example among my family members, in my church, on my job, and in my community, but I wasn't complete and the Treasure Chest of Life was not nearly empty. There was the pearl of great price, Love. A life (mollusk) had been sacrificed for each pearl, but there was one pearl that demanded my attention. Its translucent luster and its delicate play of surface colors grabbed me at the seat of my affections— the heart.

I would now know the true meaning of what it is to be a beautiful woman. I know that good mothers have that (mother wit) something special for their children. It would be proven over and over in families around the globe that we call earth. What does a good mother have that many fathers do not have? Perhaps a good mother has warm affections, labeled as motherly (maternal) love. At any rate, this pearl was for me, the Pearl of Love. I held it firmly, pressed it to my heart, and absorbed the beauty of its contents—LOVE.

LOVE IS A MORE EXCELLENT WAY

THE PEARL OF LOVE

What Can Make Me Feel This Way? Love! I am who I am, but who I am is not all about me—it's the contents of the heart that makes the difference.

To love and to be loved is worth its weight in words and deeds. It is what makes me beautiful. I love! I Care! I Share! Who could say it better than that old preacher who would say, *"For God so loved the world that he gave his only begotten Son, that whosoever believeth in him should not perish, but have everlasting life." (St. John 3:16)*

The *Pearl of Great Price* enriched my heart with love. It ripped out all hatred, envy, malice, jealousy, and strife. I knew that I had what I needed the most, and what the world needed. Although I knew from my own reading of the Holy Bible that the kingdom of heaven is like a pearl of great price and when a treasure hunter has found it, he, (she) goes and sells all to purchase it.

The Pearl of Love

Sparkling from within my heart,
Is a pearl—some folks call it love.
Others say love is a strong emotional
Feeling, or a deep passionate affection,
Some say love can be divided into
A variety of affections: Romantic love,
Companionate Love, Brotherly Love,
Maternal Love, Paternal Love, Agape Love—
It is love just the same with various
Beautiful shades of translucent
Luster—The Pearl of Love.

A GOOD HEART MAKES THE DIFFERENCE

CHARITY

I am CHARITY
I dwell in the hearts of those
Who possess me,
I care for others—
I lend a helping hand in times
Of distress,
I feed the poor,
I dress those that are naked,
I'll build a house for the homeless,
I'll do for you, that's if you
Need my presence—
I am charity

Though my tongue speak sweet melodies,
And all people praise my lips,
Yet, if I possess not the intangible
Imponderable riches of charity,
I am but an empty vessel,
Vlid of the Pearl of Life, love...

SILVER AND GOLD

Silver and Gold
O, how I made my choice,
Silver, I am refined,
Gold, I am purified,
Silver and Gold
Makes me to shine.

The words of the LORD are pure words: as silver tried in a furnace of earth, purified seven times (Psalms 12:6)

The *pearl* of humanity, God's Great Love

There is a time and a season for every purpose under the sun:
A time to fix up what you have messed up;
A time to dress up, and a time to undress;
A time to correct the wrong, and do the right;
A time to dine, and a time for pleasure;
A time to get started, and a time to wind down;
A time to study, and a time to meditate;
A time to give hugs, and a time to kiss;
A time to look in the mirror—
There is a time to be at your best;
There is a time to love, and a time to be loved;
There is a time to pray, and a time to sing;
There is a time for total praise, and a time to Let go, and let
God.

LOVE

All around the room I roam,
Bringing sweet cheers to brighten the day.
All around the house I go,
Imparting myself to one and all.
All around the town, on every street,
Avenues and boulevards lifting a banner
Of friendship and kindness to one and all.

Crown me with respect, and decency.
Crown me with gentleness, and meekness.
Crown my head with the royal crown of life,
Let me honor my body, this earthly house,

By the life, I am now crowned to live.

The Treasure Chest of Life now beckoned my attention to more precious gems. There they were, radiantly shining right in the midst of the gold, diamonds, and silver. These magnificent gemstones set my heart ablaze with fervor as I caught sight of them.

LOVE ME TENDERLY

Love me tenderly,
You knight of my heart,
And duke of my passion,
You hold the torch,
Let the flames burn through
Rain, wind, sleet, or snow.

Love me tenderly,
Place a rose on my pillow,
And lay a bottle of wine
At my feet—
Caress me—hold me
At dawn, and at midday, and
In the dusk, let me be in the
Presence of your arms—
Submerge me in your passion
Of love, until death do us part.
This is a poem for women in love.

MY HEART! MY HEART!

My heart full of love,
Seated on its throne of
Compassion, governing my
Affections with the royal crown
Of charity, bearing the emblems
Of hope and faith—devoted to care,

Bursting with the flavor of joy—
Emanating merrily from the heart,
Words of grace, encouragement,
And comfort.

A GOOD HEART IS A GREAT WEALTH

FINDING THE MOST VALUABLE THINGS IN LIFE

On my voyage of discovery, I found the Treasure Chest of Life. I helped myself to the riches it had to offer. The true riches of life are not the trivial tangible things that so easily mislead us. It is those precious Jewels of Life that we find within ourselves that makes our life worth the toil. Of course, our lives are made so much easier when we have financial success or prosperity, and some tangible blessings that allow us to enjoy what those in abject poverty cannot afford. But even those in abject poverty can have a bit of wealth, the "Jewels Of Life" that make an enjoyable, affordable voyage of life.

ADORN ME

Adorn me beautifully with the Jewels Of Life—
Crown my head with the diadem of wisdom.
Hang pearls of love about my neck—beautify
My ears with earrings of hope.

Adorn me beautifully with the Jewels Of Life—
Place on my fingers golden rings of fidelity,
Goodness, and kindness.

Adorn me beautifully with the Jewels Of Life—
Bridle my tongue with the precious stone of truth.
Paint my lips with the lipstick of innocence—
Girdle my belly with sincerity.

Shoe my feet with the sandals of decency,
And self-respect—Adorn Me.

I am dressed with life's essentials and beauties that emanates from my very being—I'm dressed up, fixed up, highly favored, and blessed.

CLUE II

DRESSING FOR THE OCCASION OF LIFE

May I now pass through the portal of time all dressed for the occasion of life. Crown me the queen of victory, with the royal diadem of Self-Respect and Decency.

I was now all dressed in fine white linen that represented purity and chastity. Although beautifully dressed, nevertheless, I longed for more.

Dressing up for life's tedious journey is a personal affair that searches the depths of each individual's mind and heart.

Dress For The Occasion

Dress my fears with Boldness,
Dress my doubts with Faith,
Dress my weariness with Patience,
Dress my pride with Humility,
Dress my shortcomings with a
Willing mind to succeed,
Dress me for the occasion.

SHOPPING TIME!

I had my share of life's jewels, now it was off to shop! I mean, shop! The modern day malls in my area caught my attention, with stores too numerous to count. I had an enjoyable task at hand. My desire was to enter the mall of my choice and go directly to the store that sold the style of garbs for the kind of woman I had become. But finding what is for me nowadays is very difficult, especially with all the various styles that are not becoming to my way of dressing. The first thing I had to do was to find within myself a made-up mind.

I needed a made-up mind with a bit of determination that would spur me on, especially, when I was in doubt of finding what I was searching for. The first store didn't have what I was looking for so I had to draw on that readiness, that willing, eager mind to continue against all odds. But when finding myself in a large number of stores without having any success, I had to draw on determination. Determination meant persistency, perseverance, and patience—I just couldn't accept anything. You should know that I am alluding to something beyond just good old shopping time.

I wanted that special DRESS that fitted my lines perfectly. It had to be "4" Rights! Right size! Right cut! Right material! Right elasticity! Yes, and how it draped my figure would have to make a statement of modesty, decency, and royalty.

The Dressing Up Adventure

Dressing up in life is part of who I am. We all dress for various occasions; but there was a need for me to shroud the beautiful person I had become in that perfect apparel. I made my considerations, and I thought about buying dresses for various events in my life.

THE MEANING OF MY DRESSES' COLORS

My dresses' colors were a must. Colors would come to be a symbol of who I had become; nevertheless, it is not the color of the dress that makes a woman beautiful. I try to find the colors within—I just love white dresses.

The four "Rights" were exploding and erupting in my mind as though Mount Saint Helens volcanic eruption had been revisited: The Right Color! Right Size! Right Style! \Right Elasticity!

THE WHITE DRESS — CHASTITY

THE WHITE DRESS, *the symbol of Chastity*, came to me with all the beauty of what white means. The *white dress* would be a symbol of purity, chastity, and innocence. The beautiful, empowered, purpose driven woman must have a white dress in her wardrobe. It is not easily kept clean; spots can be easily seen. On the other hand, what more could I say, the white dress is what I wanted, so I must do what it takes to keep it white and clean. This meant that I had to be watchful on every avenue of life and careful on every boulevard. The do's and don'ts would always be present to remind me that I'm suited in white.

White is easily spotted, stained, and soiled—watch where you sit, stand, walk, and touch!

THE PURPLE DRESS — PROSPERITY

THE PURPLE DRESS, the symbol of *Prosperity*, was no less valuable. It presented me, the wearer, a little bit of royalty. I learned to be self-sufficient, self-supporting, and prosperous. I was an empowered woman, a queen by my own rights and privileges. I was rich, or should I say, wealthy.

Wealth comes in various packages. Make the choice, considering what it is that makes you wealthy, regardless of the size of your bank account.

THE BLUE DRESS — GOOD HEALTH

THE BLUE DRESS, the symbol of *Good Health,* was a must with a lot of sincere wishes attached. What is wealth without good health? Give me the beauty of the white and purple dress, but I needed good health. A good healthy body and mind would mean that I could continue to challenge short-term and long-term goals.

Watching My Diet for Health's Sake! I learned to watch my diet, exercise, and get the kind of needed rest that would make me feel refreshed. Early to bed, early to rise, with an apple a day as a mild mannered reminder.

Doctor's Orders—my personal care physician advised me to watch my diet. This was a red flag that pointed out the kind of foods that I should scale down or not eat at all.

The Blue Dress of Good Health was on.

Weight watching, while eating healthy, arose with me each day. When the day came to an end, I knew not to stuff my stomach before going to bed.

My cholesterol and my triglycerides were smoking! I put down the wrong eating habits, and with a little help from Trilipis and Niaspan my cholesterol levels are down, and the smoke has cleared.

THE FAST FOOD COMMANDMENT

Thou shall choose wisely
The food that enters the mouth,
Or you will be sorry on
Tomorrow's awaking.
And you shall watch that
cholesterol, saturated fat,
trans fat and all the other
woes of eating.
Watch that bologna—
fried rice—you name them!
Watch That Salt!
Watch That Sugar!
Too much, too long,
Will show up and
Show out

THE RED DRESS — WOMEN IN LOVE

THE RED DRESS, the symbol of (romantic love). Women in Love was a breathtaking beauty. I have always loved red dresses, that is, when the fashions were right for me. Can you imagine being dressed in a beautiful red dress with accessories that send onlookers' eyes into stares that only can be broken by a bolt of lightning? The red dress, a symbol of romantic love, was a need. We all need a love (red dress) life. We need to hear those words that makes us feel good about who we are. "I love you. You're the best thing that ever happened to me." When romantic love, coupled with a bouquet of red roses, is accepted, it becomes an invigorating force like a burst of sunshine on a cloudy day, setting the stage of romance. Yet, I knew that love would come attached with a demand for reciprocating or should I say, be accepted and returned in a special delivery stamped package that says: I love you too—oh, true love is hard to find. The right words such as, "I love you too" is needed to complete the cycle, "He loves me, and I love him."

Waiting with Anticipation — Of course, I had long waited for the day when that old pastor of mine could consummate an agreement between me and the love of my life to be no longer two, but one in heart and mind.

Do you take "J" to be your wedded husband,
to have and to hold, to love and to cherish,
in sickness and in health, for richer for poorer,
for better or for worse, so long as you both shall live?

MARRIAGE

Marriage! Yea or Nay — Marriage is not for everybody, but for me it was the right fit. I knew that what was labeled "romantic love" had grown into companionate or affectionate love. Since romantic love (passionate love) can be short lived; don't bet your life's savings on it. It can be like a fiery inferno one day and the next day the heat of passion could be extinguished by another person who captivates your flame.

Romantic love, if placed in the right soil (receiving heart) and watered (cared after) each day, can grow into the more enduring, companionate love.

Women in (Red Dresses) love should not be misled into relationships that spell trouble from the start. You are in love now, and hope that your knight in shining armor has mutual affections.

WATCH RED FLAGS!

Red Flag # 1. Good Looks, Masculinity & Prowess

1. Don't be fooled by a handsome man's outward appearance.
    Don't judge the (man) book by its cover; read it carefully;
    The preface or introduction could be misleading.
    Read as much as you can—beware of what he has written
    with his life, and watch what he is writing!
    You are now becoming a page, or chapter, or perhaps
    a life story in his (life) book, vice versa.

"Gifts Are Blinding"

Red dresses sometimes do foolish things. Love can be blinding and downright deceiving, misleading, and an adventure that can most likely end in a shipwreck. The heart is cast upon an island of regrets, and you are left alone to decipher or ponder what made you do the thing that you vowed not to do. Let's face it! Love made you do it, but will you do it again, and then another time? That is the question.

Red Flag # 2. Disguises, Falsifications, and Acting Ability

1. Don't be fooled by his flattery, persona, etc. He could be a Dr. Jekyll, and Mr. Hyde.

You are in love, but don't let his lucrative offers or bribery with fine gifts, undermine your sense of making good decisions.

Red Flag # 3. Prosperity, Position, Power, and Prestige

1. Don't let his financial status or position of authority work over your common sense of humility.

2. Don't let his offers buy your dignity.

The Red Dress is on, but hold to your modesty and sense of who you are and how beautiful you really are.

THE PINK DRESS — FEMININITY

Pink is a color that is associated with femininity. It is introduced to baby girls via diapers, pull-ups, and the like. When I am *sold-out* on shopping for the right dress, style, and color the pink dress is not on the top of my list. It is what I would say is least purchased by me in the shopping malls. But never mind that, because to me, the pink dress is a symbol of what a real woman is. She is "woman," a softer side of creation, with a special assignment to reproduce the generation. Her position of femininity has stood the challenges of time. She has been the very centerpiece from primitive times—dominated—enslaved; but still giving what is needed to make little boys be boys and girls be girls. So, regardless of who you are, wear your pink dress. Wear it with a sense of who the Creator of life has made you.

PINK! PINK! FEMININE PINK!

Pink! Pink! Feminine pink,
Sweet girl, beautiful woman,
For now and tomorrow,
Jewels of nature,
A girlfriend,
A bride—a mother,
A dear grandmother,
All dressed in pink,
And wearing it well.

WOMEN IN DRESSES of various colors make up our homes, churches, workforce, and nations. They are present in every walk of life, wearing the dresses, gloves, shoes, and the hats (roles) for the occasion, and of course, carrying a purse that demands the attention of business owners worldwide.

WOMEN IN HATS — ROLES

I had to find the hat that matched those beautiful dresses, but one hat couldn't say it all. While some hats add to attractiveness, others detract from the appearance of the dress. I was bent on finding a hat for each dress. Finding the one hat that fits all was out of the question.

The hat is a symbol of (roles) duties, responsibilities, vocations, livelihood, etc. The beautiful, empowered, purpose driven woman so often finds herself wearing more than one hat.

Find The Accessories That Match Your Dresses.

HATS, HATS AND MORE HATS

The search was on, finding the right hat for the occasion of life was a must! I had to draw on my shopping skills and experiences, while letting my imagination take me to the hat rack where the selections tugged at my decision-making process—I was ready to go for it.

Hats are symbolic of the roles I had to play in life. Hats are here to stay. They have dressed the heads of women throughout the ages, whether just being a good mom, fixing a meal, or keeping the house looking good. Although, in various cultures, especially in the matrilineal sphere, women wear the main hat of the family. In other words, "she wears the pants." Regardless of your role in life, remember that you are beautiful, empowered, and you have a purpose driven life.

WOMAN'S HAT

A hat for my head,
A chore for my life.
A hat for my head,
A role in life to play.
A hat for my head,
Strength, Beauty, and Authority—
A woman's hat,
That is, a woman's hat.

The hat rack is of paramount importance to the empowered woman because she is aware of the authority that is associated with her position. She takes on the responsibilities that fall to her hands and musters up the courage and strength to endure the moment.

Wear your hat with dignity and respect others. On whatever

stage you may stand, be real, for the whole world is a stage and you are the actress. Dress for each scene—your stage is your plight of life. Enter onto your stage with boldness of heart and mind; don't fear the audience, you are in control. The hat was on, adding a little more beauty, defining and perfecting my efforts to remain empowered, beautiful, and purpose driven.

DRESSING THE HANDS

Now that I had found the right hat, I was off to find the gloves that made me feel like a queen dressed for the royal ball of life. Gloves weren't something that I frequently bought, yet, on some occasions, although rarely, I wanted to add that little touch of elegance to my outfits.

Gloves cover the hands. The hands are symbols of life. To cover the hands means adding a touch of beauty to life itself. All that you are, and all that you possess in life, is somehow written in the hands.

A glimpse at the hands is like looking at your purpose in life. Understanding your purpose in life gives you a broader perspective on the route that you are traveling and the road from which you have trodden.

Some gloves are designed for beauty, while others are to keep the hands warm in cold weather. Yet, there are other gloves that we wear to protect the hands when doing various jobs that may endanger the hands.

MY HANDS

My hands on the cradle,
I rock.
My hands on the stove,

I cook.
My hands on the broom,
I sweep.
My hands in the field of my endeavors,
I go.
My hands though busy, but nevertheless,
My hands I give to one and all,
Making the seasons bright.

SHOES AND MORE

Now it was time to find those special shoes and accessories that would add the finishing touch to a beautiful, well-dressed woman. Here I go again, searching for the right pair of shoes—shoes that will add that pizzazz of dressing harmony from head to toe.

When shopping for shoes, I always try to find that comfortable, perfect fit. Shoes that are too tight could easily cause an unwanted callus that will eventually cramp my day.

I LOVE THOSE SHOES

Picking the right shoes by designs and colors that match your outfit is a must. Shoes make a difference in the overall appearance of any goodly dressed woman. Shoes play an important role in the lives of women. To me, shoes are guides to our footsteps. They denote the manner of life that we lead and the pathway we tread.

I can hear that old preacher quoting from Psalms: "*The steps of a good man are ordered by the LORD: and he delighteth in his way* (Psalms 37:23)."

Beautiful shoes—beautiful walk—beautiful life.

Shoes are not easily defined, but every well-dressed woman loves them. She always tries to pick the kind of shoes that make her feel good and look good.

The beautiful, empowered, purpose driven woman is a woman of dignity and grace, with almost magical wonders and endowments. Her footsteps are ordered by a higher POWER.

"Order My Steps In Your WORD, Dear Lord"

God Is Our Shoemaker—Supply The Feet, He Will Do The Rest.

I Got Shoes

I got shoes that's for sure,
I got them on my feet,
I wear them with humility.

I got shoes that's for sure,
I got them on my feet,
I wear them with dignity.

I got shoes that's for sure,
I got them on my feet,
I wear them day by day,
Always remembering yesterday's Plight.

SHOES

Shoes on my feet,
My path I tread, inside and out,
Over those hills and mountains,
Into the valley I go with a purpose—
O, I dare not tarry.
Shoes on my feet, early before

The sunrise, or even at midnight,
When I am called upon to walk.
There is no night so dark—no day I dread,
Tomorrow I'll press on,
Regardless of the toils: for neither
Height nor depth can conquer
My footsteps — a victory in battle,
A medal of honor, a crown to wear.

I found the right shoes, but I still need some silk stockings, and perhaps a good fitting girdle, bra, and the rest of the underclothing women wear.

> *A cup full of love helps to make a better home,*
> *a better community, a better nation, and a better*
> *world.*

BEAUTY WITHIN

Dress Me II

Dress me for the occasion of life,
Prepare my garment of white linen,
Righteousness,
Embroidered with silk laces,
Integrity.
Shroud me in purple, *Royalty*—
Dress me in red, Love.
Place on my feet patent leather shoes
Of *Praise*,
Dress me for the occasion of life.

MY HANDS

My hands all dressed
In gloves—don't think
For a moment, its all
About beauty: for my
Hands are special,
A life to unfold—
Giving a comforting touch,
Holding one close to me,
Massaging an aching back,
To mend a broken heart—
Soothing wounds, and uplifting
Those that have fallen on
Life's tedious journey.

My Purse

My purse
I carry each day,
Filled with only the things that I need,
My purse.

Dresses: White, Purple, Blue, Red, and Pink—O what a wardrobe!

Stockings

Beautify my legs in stockings of silk,
Dress them for my precious moments
Of life.

Girdle

Girdle my loins with truth,
Hold my body firm each mile
That I may tread.
Be strength about my back,
And lend grace to my appearance.

Bra

O bra hold my breasts of
Sanity, let no insanity, or malice be
Dissembled within my heart.

O bra hold my breasts by day and night,
When the stranger seeks my beauty,
Hold me—my emotions you must control.

DON'T WORRY – BE HAPPY

Sometimes the path of life may become dark and dreary, but don't worry, be happy.

When troubles comes and storms doth sweep, hang on in there—don't worry, be happy. When friends are few—look up—don't worry, be happy.

MY CANDLE

O Lord, light my candle of life,
Let it burn by night and day.
Let it radiantly shine, illuminating
My path of life, giving light to each
Traveler along life's road.
Light my candle,
Let it glow with incense of love,
In the darkest night let it be a lighthouse
To those sailing life's stormy seas.
Light my candle,
Let it shine on the mountain peak,
Let it shine in the valley below,
Let it be a brilliant glow,
That shines to all far and near,
Let it shine today, and forevermore.

THIS LITTLE LIGHT OF MINE

This little light of mine,
I'm gonna' let it shine. Shine!
Shine here upon earth where
The swallows chirp—where
The eagles fly over mountains high.
I'm gonna let it shine where the
Bees buzz and the dogs bark—
Where flowers grow—all in my
Neighborhood—everywhere I go
I'm gonna let it shine, I said, I'm gonna
Let it shine. Shine!

REFLECTIONS

I had made my arrival. The mirror reflected
my outward appearance, but I knew that I had
acquired the status of the Beautiful, Empowered,
Purpose Driven Woman.

CLUE III

ENERGY, THE POWER FROM WITHIN

I was all dressed up and ready to face the challenges of life head-on. I remained focused on my purpose of life. I was enthusiastic and full of energy, which gave me the right kind of vibes. My aura would no doubt appear in beautiful colors depicting the kind of woman I am. The woman I had become was enough to make any man take notice. I imagine some men may question the identity of the beautiful, empowered woman. If they looked closely, they will find a creature of God endowed with femininity, purposed to carry on the procreation of the human race.

After I dressed up for the occasion of life; I came to the conclusion that in order to hold that well-dressed status, I would need an inward strength, a source of power and energy to keep me looking and feeling good about who I had become.

My adventure of life led me to find the Jewels of Life, the proper dresses and accessories. I wanted nothing less than to be a well-dressed woman, wearing each piece that I found with a deep and sincere appreciation of life. When the bell tolls for me to quit life's journey, I can gladly say, "I have done my best, and on the shores of eternal bliss there waits for me a more beautiful garb of light." Yet, in the meantime, I needed the kind of energy that would shine more and more each day, from sunrise to sunset.

The glow of a beautiful life emanated from within, a testimony to all that I had become—pass and present combined. The quest was now on. I had to find other inward treasures that matched what I had already become. It was a meticulously inward search, first, dressing the mind.

ENERGY OF LIFE NUMBER (1)

POWER OF THE MIND — POSITIVE THINKING

I could not fully appreciate my status of empowerment and inward beauty without a sound mind. Without it my beauty spectrum would wane and I would become like Cinderella, shivering at the sound of the clock striking midnight; her beautiful dress turning into a pauper's disgrace. Although Cinderella is a fairy tale, and I am a real living character, nevertheless, without the energy, the power of sound reasoning, I would be a wreck!

Thinking Right — Thinking is a process by which we conduct our affairs of life: business, play, etc. We formulate plans, make decisions to do or not to do, to go or not to go, to be or not to be. It is in these thought processes that our imagination meets with illusions and reality and vice versa.

THOUGHTS

Our thoughts are blueprints for deeds. They are powerful enough to persuade us to do things that perhaps we should have let go undone. Our thoughts will eventually be our deeds (actions) that lead us to gratification or regret, victory or defeat, success or failure. Having the right thoughts and making wise decisions about those thoughts will bring out the best in us. All women do not think alike, but all women should be in control of what the mind is dictating—Beware!

Women, like men, are products of their thought process. Along with energy produced by the body, soul, and spirit—a sound mind and good health are a great wealth.

Keep Good Thoughts At All Times

A powerful, positive mind makes beautiful women more beautiful, giving them an edge over women who fail to cash in on positive thinking.

Positive Thinking — Thinking positive is a must. The beautiful, empowered, purpose driven woman dresses each thought with the power of positive thinking. Her positive-charged, dressed up thoughts beautify her spoken words, giving her the power of creative wording.

MY THOUGHTS

My thoughts I carefully dress
Each day, adorning them with
Knowledge, understanding, and wisdom.
My thoughts, I carefully lay out
Within my mind, before my tongue utters
a word to a hearer's delight.
My thoughts I treasure, nursing each
One with my experiences from
Yesterday's toils and pleasures.
Although some thoughts require tender
Love and care—nevertheless, they serve my mind.
My thoughts—some are dry and distorted,
Others are full of vigor, like a refreshing rain,
Showers of blessings to guide my footsteps.
My Thoughts, I said, MY THOUGHTS.

CREATIVE WORDING

Creative wording is the power and grace of a beautiful woman's tongue. She speaks things that are positive, words that bring about desired results. She says, "It is well," instead of "It's all messed up." She says, "I can," versus "I don't know whether I can." She affirms, "I have the victory," instead of "I'm trying." "I am a winner, "instead of" I'm losing, or someday I may win."

Think It! Speak It! Believe It!

Her words are empowered by her powerful faith and trust in a higher power. I can hear my pastor preaching: "Speak to the mountain. Say, move mountain move, get out of my way, and look for it to move."

After I had finished dressing my mind with the power of positive thinking, I had to search the seat of my affection—the heart. I wanted my heart to be able to express itself in unselfish love. The preacher would say: "Be filled with charity, love one and all." I already experienced romantic love and I knew it to be a little bit selfish. It could get out of control without sending a fair warning or sounding an alarm. O yes, brotherly love was the preacher's favorite subject. Some people put a strain on your efforts to love them. I realize the beautiful, empowered, purpose driven woman must have a healthy portion of love. She must have fervent love that will make her shine radiantly, even at times when there is no reciprocity.

ENERGY OF LIFE NUMBER 2

POWER OF THE HEART — LOVE

The beautiful, empowered, purpose driven woman cannot unveil her true beauty unless the heart has the power to generate the kind of electricity that gives her that special heart fervor. The heart fervor is the inner power source that transfigures an already beautiful person into a magnificent representative of the human species.

The empowered, purpose driven woman has beautiful qualities in her heart, exemplified in unselfish acts of charity. My preacher would say: "Have faith, hope, and charity, but the greatest of these is charity."

CHARITY BEGINS IN THE HEART

PERFUMES

Oh, how I like to smell good. Perfumes come in various packages. Sometimes it can be fantastic fragrances that grab at the sense of smell, sending the nose on an "I love that scent" adventure. It can be a fragrance that says, "not this, it is too bold of an adventure." The old saying: "beauty is in the eye of the beholder" should be considered when testing perfumes, but it should be changed to: "the fragrance is in the nose of the sniffer." My favorite perfumes may not be what other women like.

Finding the right perfume is a challenge but, believe me, the perfume that fits your sense of smell is out there waiting on you.

COSTLY PERFUMES

From the bottle of the most costly perfume to the bottle of the soul—I had now found the sweet spice of life, the perfume that makes a well-dressed, empowered, purpose driven woman, queen for the day. It was all there. It was all beautiful. it was all fulfilling. It was all that I needed. I found the right perfume, the perfume of a super rich and rewarding life. The perfume was cheerfulness, coupled with happiness, and freedom from many of humankind imperfections.

The *perfume of life* is that fragrance of life that makes us beautiful. Pour it on heavily and wear it each day.

All that we say or do makes up how we smell to others.

THE PERFUME OF RIGHTEOUSNESS

The perfume of a good life is when we are free from the odor of sin.

Most women will try on perfume—having the right perfume makes a big difference. A beautiful, well-dressed woman with a bad smelling perfume will find it difficult to make good impressions.

As a beautiful, empowered woman, I had what I wanted. It was now time to put it all together: the jewelry, the fabulous dresses, the magnificent hats, the shoes and all. . . .

SMELLING

Smelling good each inch of the way,
Foot by foot, the whole mile.
Smelling good in the morning,
And at midnight let fragrances
Be smelled as you close your eyes
In a slumbering sleep—
Wake up smelling good,
And someone will notice,
Although their tongue may not express it.

MY CHOICE OF CLOTHING

My closet was now full of a choice selection of clothing that fitted me perfectly. It was now left up to me to keep my wardrobe in tiptop shape and looking like new. But I knew things often changes, and that there was no constant, but change itself. I had enjoyed wonderful life experiences, all mingled with some experiences that I wanted to forget. Life does not deal us a straight hand all the time, in other words, sometimes we have to swallow a few bitter pills.

Good Days And Bad Days — Having some good days, and bad days makes up our walk of life. However, when I weigh my days on the scale of my existence, my good days out weigh my bad days, so I say, "I won't complain."

STRENGTHS AND WEAKNESSES

Knowing my strengths and weaknesses is a must! How strong am I? What would it take to break me down? Where is my weakness? Do not be like Samson of the Bible, who was blessed with great strength, but had weaknesses that ultimately brought him to shame and finally to a sacrificial death. You must know your limitations. Beware! Your strengths are not without challenges. Your challenges may arise out of insecurities or from external sources. They are there, just waiting to test your stamina. Stay dressed up and looking good. In light of the whole matter, I am all dressed up and wearing the right clothing for the right occasions.

A Sense Of Choice — The choice was mine. I took a glimpse at my wardrobe and was humbled by its significance and symbolism. The white dress, *chastity*, I wore with humility. The purple dress, *prosperity*, gave me a sense of power. The red dress was a moment to experience *love*, but still I held on to my godliness and dignity. I certainly had to cherish the pink dress, a symbol of my *femininity*.

My wardrobe gave me the kind of edge that I needed—I was dressed in the "4" rights. . . .

PUTTING IT ALL TOGETHER

While putting it all together, I found that life was not without its pros and cons, its ups and downs, as well as its valleys, hills, and mountains. The ups, the downs, the valleys, the mountains are all there, making you who you are. I heard my pastor say, "It is in the valley that we grow." Not that I prefer valley type experiences, but sometimes our valleys make us strong. I realize that a valley is only a depression between two slopes. In the valley I sing and pray. On the mountain my songs and prayers never cease.

PUT IT ALL IN THE MASTER'S HAND

MAKING THE RIGHT CHOICES IN LIFE

Life is like a box of chocolates, make a choice—taste it before eating it!

CHOCOLATE

Chocolate! Dear Chocolate,
Chocolate, sweetie, Chocolate
Chocolate, sugar, Chocolate,
Chocolate, honey, Chocolate,
Chocolate, chocolate, chocolate,
Each piece a treat, each piece,
An event of life—
The sweet crave is satisfied,
The appetite is quenched,
When the flavor is just right—
A life well chosen, lived to
Its fullness, sweeter than my
Chocolate treats.

I made my choice and was determined to stick with it—but is life simple as making a choice selection out of a box of chocolates? If it is, I certainly would pick the pieces with the best taste. For the most part, our choice of taste differs. Sometimes we become victims of our own taste. We become victims of what we like and dislike. By the way, we are products of nature and nurture, and every other known and unknown thing in our environment that makes us who we really are.

The Serenity Prayer

"God, grant me the SERENITY
To accept the things I cannot change,
COURAGE to change the things
I can, and the WISDOM to
Know the difference."

DOING IT RIGHT THE FIRST TIME

I had done it right. I felt good about myself; nevertheless, I had to employ a mild mannered friend, "*Caution*," to keep me watchful. Surely, I was dressed up for my moment of life. I had all that I needed to make the voyage of life; but life is not so simple. It is a complex system that needs common sense, knowledge, understanding, and wisdom to keep it intact and on track.

DAY BY DAY

Each day has its own way of dealing with who you are. Some days, perhaps, you are greeted by a serene twenty-four-hour-a-day of inner peace and harmony. The things or events that occur on your pathway, you might count them as blessings. On the other hand, there are upside down, twenty-four hour, knockout days when everything appears to be a crashing disaster, breaking the sweet serenity of the day.

STAYING BEAUTIFUL AT ALL COST

Staying beautiful and powerful needs no introduction—it is who you are. It is the sum total of all your being. The toes of the feet, the fingers of the hands, and all other body parts tell the story about who you are:

YOUR LIFE IS YOUR TREASURE

You are beautiful, it's who you are. You must stay the course—beautiful.

YOUR HEALTH IS YOUR WEALTH

REFLECTIONS

Now, that I was queen for a day, all dressed in my best— inwardly—I had it altogether—I was ready, willing, and able to accept my role on my pathway of life.

TAKE A GOOD LOOK IN THE MIRROR

The mirror gives out a reflection of the entity that stands before it. It cannot tell whether they are good, bad, beautiful, or what some folks may call ugly. One very sensitive woman as she strode past me, watched me as I stared deeply into a dressing room mirror. She paused and said, "The mirror don't lie." I replied, "The mirror can't see what's on the inside, therefore it could be misleading, or even lying." I further explained that the mirror can't see beyond the cover. Hold a book up to a mirror and all you will see is the cover. The cover does not reflect the character of each page when (read) perused.

Looking Good — I was looking good and I knew it. The mirror reflected how I dressed myself. A well-dressed woman knows the combination has to fit and work for her. From her hairstyle to the shoes on her feet, it all has to work in harmony for that special dressed up moment of life.

WHAT THE MIRROR DOESN'T SHOW

I was dressed up by my "know how," but in a sense, I knew that the outward appearance could mask what had been implanted and cultivated within. That inward beauty that I acquired over the years would emerge, whether or not I was in the presence of family members, friends, or foes.

Dress up the mind and heart—look your best each day

WHAT YOU SEE IS NOT ALWAYS WHAT YOU GET

I could have been fooled many times over by the appearance of others, but here again, I called on the wise old preacher who taught me not to look on the outward appearance but look on the heart. The outward appearance can be deceiving, an elusive snare to catch wandering eyes that fail to recognize the crucial flaws concealed by flesh and bones.

The beautiful, empowered, purpose driven woman must always hold her ground. She must not let go of her dignity, illustrious character, and every other good thing that makes her who she is.

O LORD, HELP ME TO STAND; HELP ME TO HOLD ONTO THE BEAUTY OF HOLINESS.

The beautiful, empowered, purpose driven woman is a woman of dignity, and grace. She has an almost magical persona that enshrouds her, creating a beautiful aura that is intensified by her deportment. She is the woman of the hour, building on each minute, that makes her a special presentation of the day.

THE MIRROR'S TELLTALE SIGN

While staring in the mirror I saw a reflection of me, my face, a face that had the telltale signs of the Treasures of Life that I had accumulated over the years. I stared deeply within the very framework and fabric of my mind, trying to decipher the stuff that makes me who I am. I could see signs of the strong women that helped to mold me into the person that I am today. There was my mother with her ability to endure suffering; my grandmother who could render a cure for pains and woes without having any former education. My grandmother was a physician, a medical doctor, not by choice, but by necessity. There were countless other women who I had an indelible brush with. They were encounters of the best kind that left me with an inheritance of strength and beauty.

But what I could see in the mirror were only faint shadows of past experiences that represented only a minute part of all my experiences. My ancestors and other great women were now intermingled with who I am today. I took a little dignity and common sense from my father's cup, a little patience, from my mother's jar, a little boldness from my aunt's plate, and a little ingenuity from the family's pot—little values—a treasure that helped to make me who I am.

THE EYE PROBE

Probing deeply within my mind, I could see cause-and-effect, seen and unseen forces, things that undoubtedly struck me like I was a piece of metal yielding itself before the driving force of a blacksmith's hammer. The results would be seen throughout my life in all that I set my hands to do. I could discern, with a sense of appreciation, some of the marvelous things that were now a built-in mechanism of pure virtue. I saw within myself the wheel of experiences and all those experiences worked on me. I knew that both good and bad encounters made me. *I stared deeply.*

THE BLACKSMITH

I am a "plowshare"
Whet me by the blow of your hammer.
Sharpen me on your anvil,
Bend me to righteousness,
Mold me to steadfastness,
I am in your hands.
Make me to be a woman
Of strength and beauty—
Place me in the flames,
Shape me for life's tedious journey.
Mix me with the right kind of
Metals until I am strengthened.
Overlay me with pure gold, the
Gold of faith and power,
And when I am done,
Send me to the Jeweler. . . .

O Jeweler, dealer of precious gemstones,
I yield myself to you,
From the blacksmith's anvil I came ready
For you to inlay precious stones,
Gemstones, most beautiful—
Set in my heart a diamond of charity,
A ruby of hope,
A sapphire of truth,
A jasper of dignity,
A pearl of love,
Then, I shall plow the field
Of my life with expectations
And joy—enjoying life's most precious
Treasure - life itself.

BEHOLD MY FACE

While I continued to behold my face in the mirror; I was summoned by my thought processes to analyze the beauty of my strength and to calculate the sum total of who I had become—the calculations were astounding. The math had done its job, and I was left spellbound, knowing that each part of me, was nothing less than a mere fraction of small parts working in harmony with body, soul and spirit.

BODY AND SOUL

Body, most beautiful,
Yield your substances to the soul,
Soul that lies within,
Create a harmony of will,
O Soul! Soul! Soul!
Soul, the essence of all that I am,
The inner me, all dressed for heavenly bliss,
Guide my mind, caress my emotions,
Be an eternal flame within,
A divine entity purged from the
Iniquities of the body.

I wanted to be a beautiful, empowered woman endowed with all the making of a princess. I wanted my head crowned with the royal diadem of dignity and my body draped in royal (fashions) apparels—stately—I stretch forth my scepter of power and independence to all those who come near.

The mirror was working on me, the very essence of my being. But then I noticed there were faint lines on my face, signs of a woman that had aged. Like aged wine, I had become a better woman, an epitome of womanhood. Nonetheless, that is beside the point. Some of us women like to apply a little make-up when needed.

ENJOY EACH DAY—BE THANKFUL

PUTTING ON COSMETICS

I shopped for all that I needed to make me a beautiful, empowered woman in my cycle of life, but there was a pressing need to find the right cosmetics. Cosmetics can hide unwanted impressions by beautifying the physical body. At the same time, cosmetics reveal a little about the character of the wearer. Finding the right cosmetics is a must. Cosmetics should have the kind of ingredients that gives them the right texture and fragrance. The texture must be pleasing to the touch and the fragrance pleasing to my olfactory organ, the nose. They must work in harmony with my skin to enhance the feeble parts of my face or other body imperfections.

Those old gospel preachers years ago wouldn't allow women to wear make-up in church. Lipstick alone would've pronounced a cry, like this: "She is dressed like Jezebel." Nowadays, women are free to exercise their right to wear modest make-up in church. But I am not really alluding to the outward appearance, I want make-up for inward beauty, that is, the make-up of a strong mind and heart.

Make-Up

Make up my face with the cream of respect,
Build a foundation on decency,
Put on the mascara of chastity,
Line my eyes with foresight,
Paint my lips with the rouge of love
Make up my heart, O Lord,
With the beauty of your presence,
Instill within the center of my affection,
A fountain of love, and help
Me to draw from this fountain

The precious water of sharing
And caring—charity—Make-Up.

LINES, CROW'S FEET, AND WRINKLES

I observed my face in the mirror. Mirror, mirror on the wall. Who's the fairest one of all? Yes, I could see a few faint lines slowly evolving and someday would become wrinkles. I was watching out for crow's-feet, not noticeable, but perhaps someday would make their appearance on each side of my face. Wrinkles are nothing to be ashamed of, that is, if you have spent your younger days with discretion and prudence. Each facial line is a telltale sign of a person that has lived and experienced life. There is no way around growing old, except the grim reaper (death) of souls.

BEAUTIFUL FACIAL LINES

The beautiful lines of longevity swept me away. They arose and spoke to my mind, uttering a voice of complete resolve: *Your youth was like a beautiful rainbow illuminating an ominous sky.* I must admit that the showers of God's blessed hand had fallen upon me and like a plant, I grew graciously, bore fruit, and taught my children the golden rule.

My youth was fading with time. I knew that I had a time to be born and a time to die; but this was the time I wanted to live and experience life itself. . . .

I had made great strides. Achievement became my trademark of excellence. Excellence was by no means left alone by itself. There were aspirations, determination, and that indomitable spirit to succeed and be the best.

Being The Best — Being the best needed: determination, perseverance, patience, and footsteps ordered by the Lord. I held on to hope when in despair. I wrestled impatience with patience, and the mind to quit, I submerged in a driving force of continuity.

DETERMINATION

I ride upon the wings of determination,
And embrace the gold of life, patience—
I rest in the arms of hope.
I am determined not to waver—
I am not to be a slave of frustration—
Upon my throne of courage, I govern my day
Humility, mercy, and grace makes my scepter
I am determined.

DON'T QUIT

Don't quit I said,
Make one more step,
One step won't take you very far,
So keep on stepping—
Your prize is just ahead,
Although you may grow tired,
Remember there is always
Rest for the weary, and the burdens
Of life are only for a season.

I AM NOT TO BE

I am not to be, I am not to be broken.
I am not to be, I am not to be cast down.
I am not to be, I am not to be conquered—
Victory is my design,
Courage is my shield,

Faith is my daily meal,
I cash in on hope, while I bend my
Knees in prayer.

LOOK AT ME

I was created in the image and likeness of God. I am some-body. You are somebody! Your perspective of life may differ. Your likes and dislikes may not be all the same. But you must find those beautiful qualities in others and use them as building blocks in your life—Look At Me!

Look at me,
My eyes are emeralds of respect,
My lips are golden bars of wisdom,
They tell the story of knowledge and understanding.
Fasten your eyes upon me,
And stare me in the face,
I am your example—Look at me!

A WOMAN SOLDIER

She faces each battle with courage, and fortitude,
She is the captain that gives the commands,
She is the sergeant that leads the platoon,
She is the corporal, the foot soldier that fights
For justice, fair-play and equity.
She is the flag bearer that holds the banner high,
Regardless of the heat of the battle, or the rough terrain.

DESIGNED TO WIN

The Beautiful, Empowered, Purpose Driven Woman
Is designed to be a winner.
She stands upon her good morals and principles

That makes her beautiful.
She is a guide to her family, a role model that exemplifies
what it takes for others to navigate through the labyrinth
of life.
She is a star by her own right, and holds her own
regardless of circumstances.
She is designed to win.

BE A WINNER—THE BATTLE IS THE LORD'S

THE WOMAN STAGE

The stage is set,
Each day a scene, an act—
She is superb, an eloquent performer.
Each day is a scene, an act of dignity
In her home, church, and community.
She dresses for the spectators, and
Is applauded by the audience.
She is in command, ready, willing, and beautiful
Integrity is her mark of excellence.
She is glamorous in character,
A woman with purpose,
Empowered from within—
She plays her part well.

TO BE OR NOT TO BE

To be or not to be born.
To be or not to be a woman of purpose.
To be or not to be a woman of inward beauty.
To be or not to be a woman of dignity.
To be or not to be ensnared by frivolity,
To be or not to be a slave to foolishness—
To be or not to be godly in appearance—

A sculpture of a real woman among myriads.

KEEP THE FAITH

Through life's horrific storms
Keep the faith, and press on.
Mountains may appear insurmountable,
Keep the faith, and keep on climbing.
The rivers may seem insuperable,
Keep the faith, and don't give up.

I AM A QUEEN

I am a Queen,
Beautifully adorned,
All dressed for the royal ball of life.
I am in my royal carriage of time—
The banquet of life is my table—
The parade of life is in progress—
I raise my scepter of power, and humbly
I bow my head for golden moments
Of a life orchestrated by the King of
Kings. . . .

I am queen of my life,
Governor of my will,
President of my status,
I am queen at the dawning of day,
I am queen at the setting of the sun,
I am queen now and forevermore.

CHARITY

I am Charity standing at the door,
Reaching out to a stranger in dire
Times of need.
I am Charity sitting at the table,
Feeding the hungry.
I am Charity walking for paupers who lost
Their support of life.
I am Charity whispering words of
Comfort to those that need consoling.
I am Charity holding an umbrella in times of
Rain when others would be wet by troubles,
Or temptation's hidden snares.
I am Charity in the morning,
I am Charity at noon,
I am Charity in the evening,
I am Charity in the midnight hours,
All the daylong.

ABCs FOR WOMEN

Avoid the path of the ungodly.
Be alert at all times.
Care for those who are in need.
Doubt should not be entertained.
Eat the words of the wise.
Faith is the steering wheel.
Goodness should prevail over evil.
Hold to God's unchanging hand.
In God put your trust.
Joy of the Lord is your strength.
Kisses of gratitude to each day earned.
Love your neighbor as yourself.
Make up your day with integrity.
Note each day as blessed.
Open your mind to wisdom.
Pause to see where the day is taking you.
Quit bad habits.
Resist temptation.
Stop and rest when needed.
Trust in the Lord with all your heart.
Understanding should be a companion.
Victory is yours to have.
Watch and Pray.
X out things you don't need.
You are in control of your mind.
Zap out frustration and depression.

Though I speak with the tongues of men and of angels, and have not charity, I am become as sounding brass, or a tinkling cymbal. Apostle Paul

The sum total of the whole matter is to fear God and keep his commandments. Ecclesiastes

YOU FINISHED TO BEGIN

BEAUTICIAN

O sweet beautician, Jesus, thy spirit be,
I came to thee with a head full of unkempt hair,
Each strand gave thee no praise,
I was wretched, and undone—
My clothing slouched: for I had no
Girdle to hold me fast—I was a mess.

O sweet, beautician, thy spirit be,
Wash my head with pure water,
Sit me under the dryer for a moment of peace,
Straighten each strand of hair to thy delight,
Make me beautiful, my beautician be,
Let me look into the mirror of thy
Amazing Grace—
Shine the light of thy countenance upon
My weary face—
My eyelids now reflect thy presence,
My eyebrows sing of thy mercy,
My lips are painted with roses of love
from above—
I am beautified, my beautician, be.
Beautician.

List your strengths and weaknesses.